MAAH KHAN

Know the Difference: Old Age Forgetfulness or Is it Dementia?

This book was professionally typeset on Reedsy.
Find out more at reedsy.com

I am dedicating this book to my Mom

Contents

1

Introduction

Do you know the difference between old age forgetfulness and Dementia? I didn't. It had never crossed my mind to sit down and think about my aging parents and what tools and resources I needed to help them as they age. Since my childhood, I have seen both sides of my grandparent's age and had normal old-age forgetfulness. With my busy life and family, I just didn't think until it crept up on me. I felt so helpless and frustrated with the lack of knowledge I had.

My dad's passing away took a great physical and mental toll on my mom. Her health started to go down. Her anxiety and depression doubled and she was seen crying and begging God to take her to my dad. No matter what we did, nothing worked to calm her down.

After my dad's death, my mom sold the house, another shock for her, and moved in with my brother in a different state. She stayed there a few years and then decided to come and live with us. We hit it off instantly and she chose to stay here for the rest of her life. She stayed with us for 11 years. Those were the best bonding times for her and me.

I loved and enjoyed every moment of those 11 years. Sure we had our ups and downs but we never let it last longer than a few minutes. We always brushed them off.

My mom was my role model with her strength, courage, patience, and dealing to smile in any situation she walked through. Very organized and a great mom and wife. Don't let me forget a great cook too. When she started complaining about forgetfulness I thought "Oh she is getting old" it will be ok. It is just small minor things she is forgetting.

However, her complaints started to become very obvious and frequent. First, I brushed it off thinking she was overdoing it. She is trying to get my attention. However, her behavior was getting very odd. She started to hallucinate and tried many times to escape the house. I had to put chairs and boxes in front of the door every night to stop her. At this time I decided to get help and told her doctor about her condition and her behavior.

The results came and it was then I learned dementia has sneaked into her brain and taken control. I felt like my whole world came crumbling down from all directions. How could this happen? My mom is my role model. It was very shocking for me when the realization hit me that my mom, the strong pillar of our family, was becoming like a small child. I decided to keep her at home and become her full-time caregiver. While I was learning about what dementia is and how to cope with it. My mom had a stroke which left her with more memory loss, her right side paralyzed, and slurred speech. As the days went by she lost the mobility to walk with a walker and started to have bladder incontinence.

She forgot who I was and started to believe I was a nurse and she was in the hospital. My mom forgot the years of her life she had spent with

2

my dad. All she remembered was the time of her childhood. She would talk about her mom, dad, and her siblings. Every time I go sit with her, she would tell the same story like a broken record of her childhood over and over again with the same enthusiasm. Laughing at her own jokes. I would just sit there, listening and playing along like this is the first time I am hearing the story.

She loved her tea time with biscuits in the evening as she called it. One day I came to get the plates back. I heard her talking so I stood in the doorway and watched her playing tea with her imaginary friend. When she saw me she offered me make-believe tea to me. There was no point telling her nobody was there besides the two of us. It was real for her and just saying those words would have been devastating for her. We had a good time at the tea party.

Later on, her appetite decreased so much that she stopped drinking tea and eating full meals. Just snacks and fruits. She loved bananas. We shared lots of laughs and tears together. She passed away in December 2021. I love you and miss you, mom. You will always be in my heart.

I chose to write this book to spread knowledge, awareness, and understanding between old age forgetfulness and dementia. So people can take action early in the process of dementia and get help to delay memory loss. This is a reference book easy to grab in time of need. Instead of searching the internet for hours and hours or days and days. I know that is what I have done.

2

What is Aging and What effects does it have on memory?

Aging is a natural process of the life cycle. As we get older our body as well as the brain goes into changes that lead to slow memory. Our brain starts to shrink in our 30s and 40s but when we are in our 60s our memory loss increases in a fast phase.

With these changes, there is a high chance that stroke, memory loss, and dementia could rise. Often people start to forget

- the names of family members or important information
- where they keep the keys
- Have a hard time with multitasking
- Not able to focus or pay attention

A healthy lifestyle, diet, and exercise can be the best defense against both physical and mental changes of an aging brain. Making small changes and making them into a daily routine will help you function better through the aging process.

- Managing blood pressure
- Healthy diet
- Exercise
- Cognitive activities
- Being socially active
- Less stress
- Heart health
- Control over depression
- Manage diabetes

Causes of memory loss in elderly

Lack of sleep

- Lack of sleep is one of the causes for memory loss. It affects reasoning and executive functioning.

Medications

- As we age we depend on medicines for all joint pains and other health issues. Most medicines cause memory loss as a side effect.

Lack of Exercise

- Lack of exercise has a negative effect on those who aren't active: "Not walking or doing other aerobic exercises on a regular basis can cause brain shrinkage and lead to small injuries to the parts of brain cells that connect with other brain cells," says Mary Ellen Quiceno, a neurologist and researcher in Dallas.

Diabetics

- Memory loss and general cognitive impairment, which are linked to type 2 diabetes. Damage to the blood vessels is common in people with diabetes which lead to cognitive problems and vascular dementia.

Vitamin deficiency

- Vitamin B12 deficiency is known to be a cause of cognition and memory loss along with a sensation of tingling and numbness.

Stroke

It is proven that stroke causes memory loss. These are the symptoms of memory loss you might experience after a stroke:

- Confusion or problems with short-term memory
- Wandering or getting lost in familiar places
- Difficulty following instructions
- Trouble making monetary transactions

Depression and Anxiety

- Depression and anxiety are very common in old age. "When you're depressed, the serotonin levels in your brain decrease and this can affect attention, processing speed and memory consolidation, causing a 'pseudodementia' of depression," says neurologist Richard Isaacson, director of the Alzheimer's Prevention Clinic at Weill Cornell Medicine and New York-Presbyterian Hospital

3

Natural Aging vs Dementia

I n this section, we will learn the difference between natural aging vs Dementia. Check below for some examples that are given but please note that this is not a diagnostic tool.

Natural Aging memory impairment

- Small unnoticed disruptions in daily life,
- Having difficulty completing tasks as you are used to doing.
- Getting very difficult to learn and remember new things
- Most importantly there's no underlying medical condition that is causing your memory problems.

Dementia

Dementia is a disease of the brain. It attacks the memory. With dementia the memory loss is so severe to the point where:

- It interferes with your daily life and makes it very hard unable for

you to stick to your normal routine,
- It's very difficult to learn new things
- You're forgetting to do the daily tasks you're familiar with
- Forgetting where the car is park
- Losing car keys
- Losing track of time
- Forgetting how you got to where you are
- Struggling with words, or confusion about what to say next, it may be a sign of more serious memory loss.
- Withdraw from family and friends
- Your condition has become very obvious to others.

4

7 Stages of dementia

Stages of Dementia

Please find a chart of 7 stages of Dementia Deterioration

Global Deterioration Scale (CGS) / Reisberg Scale			
Diagnosis	Stage	Signs and Symptoms	Expected Duration of Stage
No Dementia	Stage 1: No Cognitive Decline	– Normal function – No memory loss – People with NO dementia are considered in Stage 1	N/A
No Dementia	Stage 2: Very Mild Cognitive Decline	– Forgets names – Misplaces familiar objects – Symptoms not evident to loved ones or doctors	Unknown

12

7 STAGES OF DEMENTIA

No Dementia	Stage 3: Mild Cognitive Decline	– Increased forgetfulness – Slight difficulty concentrating – Decreased work performance – Gets lost more frequently – Difficulty finding right words – Loved ones begin to notice	Average duration of this stage is between 2 years and 7 years.
Early-stage	Stage 4: Moderate Cognitive Decline	– Difficulty concentrating – Forgets recent events – Cannot manage finances – Cannot travel alone to new places	Average duration of this stage is 2 years.

		– Difficulty completing tasks – In denial about symptoms – Socialization problems: Withdraw from friends or family – Physician can detect cognitive problems	
Mid-Stage	Stage 5: Moderately Severe Cognitive Decline	– Major memory deficiencies – Need assistance with ADLs (dressing, bathing, etc.) – Forgets details like address or phone number – Doesn't know time or date – Doesn't know where they are	Average duration of this stage is 1.5 years.

7 STAGES OF DEMENTIA

Mid-stage	Stage 6: Severe Cognitive Decline (Middle Dementia)	– Cannot carry out ADLs without help	Average duration of this stage is 2.5 years
		– Forgets names of family members	
		– Forgets recent events	
		– Forgets major events in past	
		– Difficulty counting down from 10	
		– Incontinence (loss of bladder control)	
		– Difficulty speaking	
		– Personality and emotional changes	
		– Delusions	
		– Compulsions	
		– Anxiety	

15

KNOW THE DIFFERENCE: OLD AGE FORGETFULNESS OR IS IT DEMENTIA?

Late-Stage	Stage 7: Very Severe Cognitive Decline (Late Dementia)	– Cannot speak or communicate – Require help with most activities – Loss of motor skills – Cannot walk	Average duration of this stage is 1.5 to 2.5 years.

Mild Dementia

Mild dementia is also known as the first stage, it is when an individual can function independently in daily routine. They are capable of driving and maintaining a social life. Symptoms of mild dementia are the same as old aging. There might be slight lapses in memory, such as misplacing eyeglasses or having difficulty finding the right word. This stage of dementia lasts between 2 and 4 years.

Moderate Dementia

In the middle stage of dementia or the second stage is the longest stage.

Memory loss is more severe than in the first stage. In this stage, it is common to forget personal history, personal identification, and address and could easily get lost due to confusion about where they are.

Communication becomes very difficult. It gets very easy to lose track of thoughts, and not be able to focus on conversion.

They get into Mood and behavior changes like aggressiveness, difficulty sleeping, depression, paranoia, repeating actions or words, hoarding, wandering, and incontinence. This moderate stage lasts between 2 and 10 years.

Severe Dementia

In late-stage dementia, also known as advanced dementia, is the third stage, individuals may not verbally communicate at all. Memory loss is the worst, they don't remember what happened about an hour ago. They don't remember family members' and family members' names. It's that time when they revert back to their childhood days. Their limbs give away, making it too difficult to walk, and they are not able to do daily living activities, including personal hygiene and eating. At the end of this stage, the individual is bedridden. This severe stage of dementia lasts 1 to 3 years.

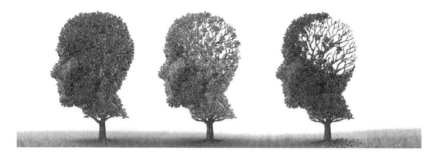

5

Treatment for Dementia

T here's no cure for dementia, but there are drug and non-drug options available to slow the progression to worsen or go to the next stage. Asking the doctor or learning about available options can help individuals living with the disease and their caregivers cope with symptoms and improve their quality of life.

Best natural cure for Dementia

- 8 glasses of water intake every day
- Walking
- Diet changes
- Try to get enough sleep
- Write down to take notes
- Read books regularly
- Try not stress
- Don't give up. Try to learn new things
- Play mental active games

Best food to eat to reduce the Dementia risk

Leafy green vegetables
These vegetables have a strong positive effect on cognitive health. Such as

1. Kale
2. Spinach
3. Cabbage
4. Collards
5. Romaine lettuce
6. Arugula
7. Leaf lettuce
8. Watercress
9. Bok choy

Non-Starchy vegetables
Have many antioxidants and anti-inflammatory compounds. It has been shown in studies that these plant antioxidants can help treat and prevent mild memory loss.

Eating more of these vegetables will keep your brain healthy. These non-starchy vegetables include

1. Broccoli
2. Cauliflower
3. Brussels sprout

Fish
Fish contains lean protein and healthy fats (omega-3). People with dementia have low levels of omega-3. Eating fish will prevent dementia and brain function.

Vitamin B-12 also comes from fish which is very essential for brain health. Low B-12 can lead to memory loss.

These types of fish have high levels of omega-3 fatty acids:

- Salmon
- Sardines
- Herring
- Mackerel
- Cod
- Tuna

Make sure to add these fish to your diet for healthy brain function.
Beans
Beans provide a good source of protein, fiber, and complex carbohy-

drates in the Dementia diet. People who eat beans once in a while are more likely to have memory loss. Make beans your regular diet.

- Green beans
- Black soybeans are two of the lowest-carb beans.

Nuts

Like fish, have lots of healthy omega-3 fatty acids. Those omega-3s will help you protect your brain health.

.A study of women over 70 has been done and found who ate 5 or more servings of nuts every week experienced better cognitive function.

Olive Oil

Olive oil is one of the most effective dementia diets. There are many other benefits as well.

The great thing about olive oil is that it contains healthy fats that your body can use as a cleaner energy source.

Monounsaturated fats, the "good" fats in olive oil, can also help you lower your total cholesterol. Eating more monounsaturated fat increases your HDL levels (good cholesterol) and lowers your LDL levels (bad cholesterol).

Poultry

As for everyone, consuming poultry is much better than eating red meat or pork. The same goes for a Dementia person. It is recommended that meat or pork should be replaced by poultry and fish to prevent further damage to memory loss.

Poultry contains lean protein which is an essential part of a diet. Make a habit of eating 1-2 servings of poultry per week. If poultry doesn't work for you then try to get protein from another source because protein is a must to have as a part of the diet.

Avocados

Avocado is a must plus to have in your diet. Another name for avocados is "SUPERFOOD" because the healthy fats in avocados provide your body with clean energy without raising your blood sugar levels.

Avocado makes the perfect salad item. Add some sliced avocado to a salad made with leafy green vegetables, beans, grilled chicken, and a handful of berries. You'll have a delicious salad that will help protect your brain, too.

Green Tea

Drinking unsweetened green tea will prevent dementia from worsening. Green tea is high in compounds called catechins. Catechins are very strong antioxidants, which are anti-inflammatory. Researchers believe that green tea is great for the brain because it has these protective properties.

Try not to sweeten your tea with anything besides zero-calorie sweeteners. Even then don't overindulge in the intake of green tea. As for unsweetened green tea, you can consume it freely.

Berries

Berries are considered a must on a diet list. Berries contain Antioxidants

- Anti-inflammatory compounds
- Fiber (a prebiotic)
- Vitamins (including vitamin C)
- Minerals

Scientific studies have found direct links between berries and brain health. One study found that participants improved their memory simply by drinking a glass of blueberry juice every day or were less likely to develop Alzheimer's if they ate more strawberries.

Make sure to add these 3 items to your diet plan Berries, fish, and leafy green vegetables to fight memory loss. Numerous studies and evidence have shown how they support and protect brain health.

Foods to Avoid for Dementia

Sugar

Try to eliminate sugar altogether from your diet because it is the main cause of inflammation in your body and brain. Chronic inflammation in the brain can lead to dementia.

Trans fats

Trans fats are man-made and they often are found in highly processed foods. Trans fats are bad for your health, including the health of your brain. They have a particularly negative effect on cardiovascular health which is linked to Alzheimer's risk.

Below find the foods that are bad for dementia

- Sugar
- Trans fats
- Typical dairy products
- High sodium

Best way to avoid trans fat is not to eat fried foods, which can be loaded with trans fats. Switching hydrogenated oils for olive oil will help, too.

Salt

Salt can raise your blood pressure and cause cardiovascular problems

24

which can turn into brain health issues. In the long run, salt intake can lead to dementia.

Try to avoid fast food or processed foods (including frozen meals), which usually contain a lot of salt

Disclaimer:

Consider PrimeHealth's Prevention Program.

We stand behind Dr. Dale Bredesen's revolutionary KetoFLEX 12/3 diet program for patients with cognitive decline. We have seen it work wonders, particularly in combination with other beneficial lifestyle changes.

As more research is published on theKetoFLEX 12/3 diet, we can't wait for more professionals and caregivers to hear about this super-effective diet plan.

6

Tips on How to Care for Dementia Individuals

Taking care of a person with dementia is not easy at all. Especially for the family. Seeing a loved one in a state of forgetting everyone or everything. It is very painful. I have been there with my mom as I have mentioned in the introduction. It takes lots of patience, perseverance, and understanding. Caregivers need to be strong physically and mentally to cope with whatever comes to them in all stages of dementia.

Some family members see these as challenges that get to be too frustrating, confusing, and heartbreaking at times. They may have many questions in their minds but don't know where to look for answers. One may ask; how can we make this easier? How can I make my home and my loved one calm and safe?

According to the Alzheimer's Association, statistics show only in the United States that 6.5 million Americans over the age of 65 live with the disease today. If no medical breakthrough or treatment is found the number could increase to 13.8 million in 2060.

For those people who want to care for a dementia person at home. Here are some helpful tips for the caregiver.

• **Don't argue**

Never argue with the person who has dementia. It will take you nowhere. They don't have the ability to think and reason. It will upset them and throw them into anxiety and depression. Try your best to divert them from the topic at hand in a nicer way.

• **Give them limited independence**

Depending on what stage the dementia person is in, if the person is capable of doing small tasks by themselves, then give a dementia patient a task to keep them occupied, a task like something that will give the mental and tactile stimulation to keep them calm.

• **Make home safe**

It is very important to make your home a safe place for people with dementia. It's really shocking to watch someone with dementia physically capable of doing something when they are determined. My mom walked very slowly with a walker and was not capable of lifting her leg to go into the stand in the bath shower stall. But at night she would climb up the chairs and step stoles to get away through the front door. Talk with the doctor and get occupational therapy and physical therapy to come for home visits. They will be able to let you know if the home environment meets the patient's needs.

- **Napping**

My mom used to stay awake all night long wandering the house looking for an escape route unsuccessfully. Thank God. But in the daytime, she would on and off take long naps all day long.

Limiting Napping time during the day is not only a good idea but a very important one too. This reduces the risk of them staying up and wandering late at night.

- **Set a daily routine**

Sitting down with a person with dementia and making a plan for the day or writing down a daily routine together will make them feel good and you can figure out what to do. Select a routine that provides meaning and enjoyment for the patient.

A daily routine is to bathe, dress, eat and go to sleep at the same time every day.

- **Make mealtime easier**

Aah! meal time. Sounds so simple and easy. Wait until you are dealing with the dementia patient. It will get very overwhelming just to get them to eat. The appetite is literally gone. I cut up fruits, vegetables, and sandwiches into small pieces to make it easy. My mom sits there and stares at the food. Just that was enough for her to fill her stomach.

I started hand feeding her, she would look at me so lovingly with her beautiful eyes but take only one bite and she is done. She would often ask me at this feeding time. Are you my mother? It was very heartbreaking hearing those words.

28

Gabriella Belacastro, a dietician with Chapters Health shared these tips to help caregivers make it easier.

- Reduce distractions. Turn off the TV and serve meals in a quiet setting.
- Distinguish food from the plate. Changes in spatial and visual abilities make it difficult for dementia patients to distinguish food from the setting. It can help to use plates or bowls that have contrasting colors with the food and table setting. Avoid patterned dishes, tablecloths, and placemats.
- Offer one food at a time. Don't overwhelm your loved one with options by loading the plate and table. For example, serve them mashed potatoes followed by the main entree.

- **Understand Sun downing**

For many family members, it is a time of dread. I would fear when it was time for sundowning. What is sundowning? It is a phenomenon that is experienced by people with dementia. It is a time when the sun goes down and day turns to night. The person starts to experience confusion, anger, and forgetfulness. The symptoms and signs to look for are crying, agitation, pacing, fear, restlessness, helplessness, anxiety, and depression.

How to avoid sundowning is simply to stick to the daily routine and distract them or keep them busy with puzzles, games, or just talk about their favorite childhood which by now you know the stories by heart.

- **Play their childhood music**

I used to ask my mom which song she likes to hear. Her answer was not a song but poetry from her childhood favorite poet. I got a poetry book for her birthday gift and would sit down with her and did my best to recite the poetry to her with her matching enthusiasm. The poems were written in her language and I had a hard time pronouncing the words she would burst into laughter commenting "silly girl ruining all the poems" but she would look eagerly waiting for me every day at the same time to come and read the poems. I think she was more into liking my company than listening to me recite the poems.

"It's amazing how many people with dementia become their old self while listening to a song they remembered as one of their favorites," shared Cramer.

A study from the University of Toronto found listening to meaningful music led to improved memory performance among early Alzheimer's patients.

7

Self-Care for caregiver

Self-care is very essential for a caregiver. From time to time it gets very overwhelming physically and mentally. You need to take care of yourself first before you take care of others. Caring for a person with dementia especially when you are the primary caregiver gets very exhausting. Every second day and night you have to be on guard. You will never know what will happen the next second. It is like living on the edge waiting and preparing yourself for the worst to come. A few times my mom tried to walk herself but fell when I was distracted by another chorus. When I heard her call my name I went to check up on her and saw her on the floor laughing hysterically. She looked at me with a confused and innocent look and said " my legs were not there. It was like someone took my legs away and ran. I kissed her on the forehead and lifted her up on her bed. She had tears rolling down her cheek and asked me "Is this how it's going to be from now on". It is no fun in the park to be a caregiver. You have to be very very strong. Take time off occasionally and go for a walk, shopping, or visit a friend.

Listed below is the resource for caregivers

1. **Respite care**

What is Respite care?

It is a short-term help for primary caregivers. It works on your schedule. It can be provided for just an afternoon or several days or weeks. The best part is for your piece of mind, it can be provided at home, in a healthcare facility, or at an adult day center.

Is Respite care covered by Insurance or Medicare?

Most Insurance plans do not cover Respite care costs but Medicare covers most of the cost for 5 days straight whether it was done in a hospital or at the health care facility. Medicaid also offers assistance

Finding respite care services

The ARCH National Respite Locator Service can help you find services in your community. In addition, the Well Spouse Association offers support to the wives, husbands, and partners of chronically ill or disabled people and has a nationwide listing of local support groups.

For more information about respite care,
National Respite Locator Service
www.archrespite.org/respitelocator
Well Spouse Association
800-838-0879
info@wellspouse.org
www.wellspouse.org
Eldercare Locator
800-677-1116
eldercarelocator@n4a.org
https://eldercare.acl.gov

Centers for Medicare & Medicaid Services

800-633-4227

877-486-2048 (TTY)

https://www.cms.gov

www.medicare.gov

This content is provided by the NIH National Institute on Aging (NIA). NIA scientists and other experts review this content to ensure it is accurate and up to date.

Resources to Relieve Caregiver Stress

iCare—online information and training for family caregivers

AARP Caregiver Life Balance website

Caregiving and Ambiguous Loss (Family Caregiver Alliance)

Ways to Take Care of Yourself (caregiver)

- Always feel free to ask for help when you need it.
- Keep a healthy diet
- Join a caregiver's support group either in person or online
- Take breaks each day. Make it a routine
- Spend time with friends or go out to your favorite place let it be gym, restaurant or store
- Take time to exercise every day
- Make regular basis visits with your doctor. Many people get so busy that they neglect their own health
- Keep your health, legal, and financial information up-to-date

Getting Professional Help

If it is getting too overwhelming and you think you can't do it anymore but you feel you are obliged to take care of the patient. It is time for you to get professional help. Mental health professionals and social workers are there to help you cope with any stress you may be feeling. They are professional and they know how to help you. They can even sit down with you and make plans for unexpected sudden events.

Mental health professionals charge by the hour. Medicare, Medicaid, and some private health insurance plans may cover some of these costs. Ask your health insurance plan which mental health counselors and services it covers. Then check with your doctor, local family service agencies, and community mental health agencies for referrals to counselors.

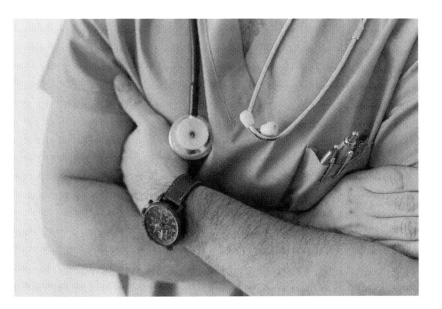

8

What If Something Happened to the caregiver?

Have you ever thought what if something happens to you while you are the primary caregiver? Who will take care of the patient? Seriously, it never crossed my mind when I was taking care of my mom, It suddenly struck me one day what if.......

It freaked me out and I started researching online and asking questions here and there until I found this article which I have decided to share here so it can be reached to people who are looking for it.

It is important to have a plan in case of your own illness, disability, or death.

- Get a lawyer to learn about setting up a living trust, durable power of attorney for health care and finances, and other estate planning tools.
- Talk with the family to decide who is willing to take responsibility for the person with dementia. Don't get discouraged if they reject that possibility. You can find more information about your local public guardian's office, mental health conservator's

office, adult protective services, or other case management services. These organizations may have programs to assist the person with Dementia in your absence.

Make a journal or notebook for the responsible person who is willing to take responsibility. Such a notebook should contain the following information.

- Emergency phone numbers
- Current problem behaviors and possible solutions
- Ways to calm the person with Dementia
- Assistance needed with toileting, feeding, or grooming

9

Advance care Planning

A dvance care planning is learning and making a decision on what type of medical care you want and letting your family and healthcare providers know your preferences. These preferences are kept as a legal document that goes into effect when you are incapacitated and unable to speak for your injury.

Research shows that advanced care planning does make a difference for a person who documents and gets the care they want from people who do not.

My parents were so organized that after my dad's passing, I went to clean their home. I went through their documents and found a bunch of advanced care planning documents for both of my parents that I never knew existed. I was so relieved to see the documents because they showed me what they prefer. I didn't have to make the hard final decisions for them.

It is a lot better to get these documents made in the early stages of dementia when the patient is capable of understanding, thinking, and can make decisions themselves.

Let's get straight to what types of decisions a person needs to make. Usually, it is an emergency treatment to keep a person alive. Doctors want to try artificial or mechanical ways to try to keep you alive. So it is time to start thinking about what kind of treatment you do or you don't want. The list is below

- **CPR**
- CPR helps restore your heartbeat when the heart stops or is in an abnormal rhythm. For young people, the heart starts beating normally after CPR but for older people, it often doesn't work due to having multiple chronic illnesses.
- **Ventilator use**
- Ventilators help you breathe. The tube is put through the throat into a windpipe so the ventilator forces air into the lungs.
- **Tube feeding, IV or fluids**
- If a person loses his ability to eat food then a feeding tube is put through the nose down to the stomach.
- If you are not able to drink, then IV fluids are put through a thin plastic tube inserted into a vein.

More important documents

There are three main documents that everyone needs to be aware of such as

- **Living will**
- In this document, you can let the doctors know what emergency treatment you want or don't want under the condition that you

are permanently unconscious and are unable to make your own decisions.

- **A durable power of attorney for healthcare**
- On this document, you will put the name of a person who has agreed to take the responsibility for the person with dementia who is under your care when you are unable to care for them.
- **Other advance care planning documents**
- On these documents, you can express your wishes about a single medical issue. Such as blood transfusion or kidney dialysis, pacemakers and ICD, etc

Advance care plan wallet card

It might be wise to carry this card in your wallet indicating that you have an advanced care plan. Here is the wallet card offered by the American Hospital Association. You can print this online and fill it out. A PDF can be found online (PDF, 40 KB).

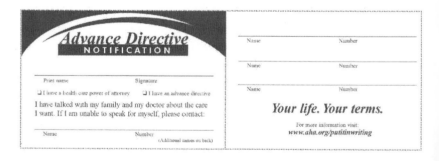

10

Conclusion

K now the difference about what is normal old-age forgetfulness and what is Dementia. It is a very thin line between the two. You will not know when dementia sneaks into someone's brain.

I wrote this book as a reference guide for people or caregivers who are going through looking for answers to so many questions like what I went through.

Please check into preparing advanced care planning. It will help when you need it most. Having an advanced care plan will give you and those close to you peace of mind. I hope people find this book to be helpful for them. That is my goal and wish to spread knowledge about what is normal forgetfulness and what is dementia?

If you find this book helpful, I'd be very appreciative if you left a favorable review for the book on Amazon!

11

Resources

Pixabay. (2021). *care*. https://www.pexels.com/search/care/. Retrieved 16 September 2022, from https://www.pexels.com/search/care/

Peters, R. (2006, February). *Ageing and the brain*. https://www.ncbi.nlm.nih.gov/pmc/articles/PMC2596698/. Retrieved 16 September 2022, from https://www.ncbi.nlm.nih.gov/pmc/articles/PMC2596698/

Fried, L. (2021, June 10). *Changes That Occur to the Aging Brain: What Happens When We Get Older*. https://www.publichealth.columbia.edu/public-health-now/news/changes-occur-aging-brain-what-happens-when-we-get-older. Retrieved 16 September 2022, from https://www.publichealth.columbia.edu/public-health-now/news/changes-occur-aging-brain-what-happens-when-we-get-older

NIA. (2020, October 1). *Cognitive Health and Older Adults*. https://www.nia.nih.gov/health/cognitive-health-and-older-adults. Retrieved 16 September 2022, from https://www.nia.nih.gov/health/cognitive-health-and-older-adults

Sadick, B. (2020, February 19). *Memory Loss Often Caused by More*

General and Reversible Health Issues. https://www.aarp.org/hea lth/brain-health/info-2020/avoiding-cognitive-decline.html?c mp=KNC-DSO-COR-Health-BrainHealth-NonBrand-Exact-29 237-GOOG-HEALTH-BrainHealth-BrainHealth-MemoryLoss- Exact-NonBrand&gclid=Cj0KCQjw94WZBhDtARIsAKxWG-8a cXrMFU6q06VzYz7fDX9_xWaNx_2ib9Pq89fDUHZ9I4CrgkAe m3AaAgpFEALw_wcB&gclsrc=aw.ds. Retrieved 16 September 2022, from https://www.aarp.org/health/brain-health/info-20 20/avoiding-cognitive-decline.html?cmp=KNC-DSO-COR-Hea lth-BrainHealth-NonBrand-Exact-29237-GOOG-HEALTH-Brai nHealth-BrainHealth-MemoryLoss-Exact-NonBrand&gclid=Cj 0KCQjw94WZBhDtARIsAKxWG-8acXrMFU6q06VzYz7fDX9_x WaNx_2ib9Pq89fDUHZ9I4CrgkAem3AaAgpFEALw_wcB&gcls rc=aw.ds

Muacevic Adler, A. J. (2020, February 13). *Low Vitamin B12 Levels: An Underestimated Cause Of Minimal Cognitive Impairment And Dementia.* Low Vitamin B12 Levels: An Underestimated Cause of Minimal Cognitive Impairment and Dementia. Retrieved 16 September 2022, from https://www.ncbi.nlm.nih.gov/pmc/artic les/PMC7077099/#:~:text=Vitamin%20B12%20deficiency%20is% 20linked,markers%20of%20Vitamin%20B12%20deficiency.

walker, T. (2018, August 20). *Can Diabetes Lead to Memory Loss?* Can Diabetes Lead to Memory Loss? Retrieved 16 September 2022, from https://www.healthline.com/health/diabetes/diabetes-an d-memory-loss#connection

American heart association. (2019, March 15). *Memory Loss.* Memory Loss. Retrieved 16 September 2022, from https://ww w.stroke.org/en/about-stroke/effects-of-stroke/cognitive-and- communication-effects-of-stroke/memory-loss

Alzheimer Society of Canada. (2022). *The differences between normal aging and dementia.* The Differences Between Normal

Aging and Dementia. Retrieved 16 September 2022, from https://a lzheimer.ca/en/about-dementia/do-i-have-dementia/differenc es-between-normal-aging-dementia

DerSarkissian, C. (2022, May 27). *Things That Raise Your Chances of Dementia.* Things That Raise Your Chances of Dementia. Retrieved 16 September 2022, from https://www.webmd.com/ alzheimers/ss/slideshow-raise-chances-dementia

The Recovery Village. (2022, April 1). *Withdrawal yahoo images.* https://www.floridarehab.com/drugs/hydrocodone/related/wi thdrawal-timeline/.

Dementia care central. (2020, April 24). *Stages of Alzheimer's & Dementia: Durations & Scales Used to Measure Progression (GDS, FAST & CDR).* Dementia Care Central. Retrieved 16 September 2022, from https://www.dementiacarecentral.com/aboutdemen tia/facts/stages/

Clark, K. (2022). *Dementia yahoo images.* Dementia Yahoo Image. Retrieved 16 September 2022, from https://images.search.yah oo.com/search/images;_ylt=AwrFRwTNiyJjn.MHNRyJzbkF;_y lu=c2VjA3NlYXJjaARzbGsDYnV0dG9u;_ylc=X1MDOTYwNjI4 NTcEX3IDMgRhY3RuA2NsawRjc3JjcHZpZAN5YjFEeGpFeU55 Nm54LjlpWXg0ZmpRZm1Nall3TUFBQUFBRGh1N0gwgwBGZyA 21jYWZlZQRmcjIDc2EtZ3AEZ3ByaWQQTjRMTGEzQkxSV2V Gb3AyeGtySlJ0QQRuX3N1Z2cDMARvcmlnaW44DaW1hZ2VzL nNlYXJjaC55YWhvby5jb20EcG9zAzAEcHFzdHIDBHBxc3RybA MEcXN0cmwDMjAEcXVlcnkDdHJlZSUyMG9mJTIwZGVtZW 50aWWEdF9zdG1wAzE2NjMyMDg0NDQ-?p=tree+of+dementia &fr=mcafee&fr2=sb-top-images.search&ei=UTF-8&x=wrt&typ e=E211US105G91648#id=6&iurl=https%3A%2F%2Fwww.marqu emedical.com%2Fwp-content%2Fuploads%2F2017%2F11%2FDe mentia_trees_-croppedjpg.jpg&action=click

Staughton, J. (2020, January 30). *17 Surprising Home Remedies For*

Dementia. 17 Surprising Home Remedies for Dementia. Retrieved 16 September 2022, from https://www.organicfacts.net/dementi a.html

Rafatjah, S. (2022, September 5). *ALZHEIMER'S DIET: 16 FOODS TO FIGHT DEMENTIA + WHAT TO AVOID.* ALZHEIMER'S DIET: 16 FOODS TO FIGHT DEMENTIA + WHAT TO AVOID. Retrieved 16 September 2022, from https://primehealthdenver.com/alzhei mers-diet/

Tentis, D. (2021). *cooked meat with vegetables.* Pixals Images. Retrieved 16 September 2022, from https://www.pexels.com/ph oto/cooked-meat-with-vegetables-725991/

Pexels images. (2021). *Fries and Burgers on plate.* Pexels. Retrieved 16 September 2022, from https://www.pexels.com/ photo/fries-and-burger-on-plate-70497/

Mudd, A. (2022, June 30). *Caring for dementia patients.* Caring for Dementia Patients. Retrieved 16 September 2022, from https://w ww.chaptershealth.org/chapters-of-life-blog/medical-conditio ns/caring-for-a-dementia-patient-10-most-important-tips-for-family/?gclid=Cj0KCQjwmouZBhDSARIsALYcouqio6GohJC0V 10WPMQeGepHp7A7z34lEtYqOJBpwG_mKzRqhsz2aMYaAsOL EALw_wcB

NIH. (2017, May 1). *What is Respite care?* Retrieved 16 September 2022, from https://www.nia.nih.gov/health/what-respite-care

NIH. (2017b, May 17). *Alzheimer's Caregiving: Caring for Yourself.* Retrieved 16 September 2022, from https://www.nia.nih.gov/he alth/alzheimers-caregiving-caring-yourself

Piacquadio. (2019, April 8). *Joyful adult daughter greeting happy surprised senior mother in garden.* Pexels Image. Retrieved 16 September 2022, from https://www.pexels.com/photo/joyful-adult-daughter-greeting-happy-surprised-senior-mother-in-ga rden-3768131/

Grabowska, K. (2020, March 10). *Crop doctor with stethoscope in hospital*. Pexels Images. Retrieved 16 September 2022, from https://www.pexels.com/photo/crop-doctor-with-stethoscope-in-hospital-4021779/

NIH. (2018, January 15). *Advance Care Planning: Health Care Directives*. Retrieved 16 September 2020, from https://www.nia.nih.gov/health/advance-care-planning-health-care-directives

Jutzeler, S. (2018, July 10). *Strawberries and Blueberries on glass bowl*. Pexels Image. Retrieved 17 September 2022, from https://www.pexels.com/photo/strawberries-and-blueberries-on-glass-bowl-1228530/

Made in the USA
Middletown, DE
17 May 2023

30756971R00031